T0201543

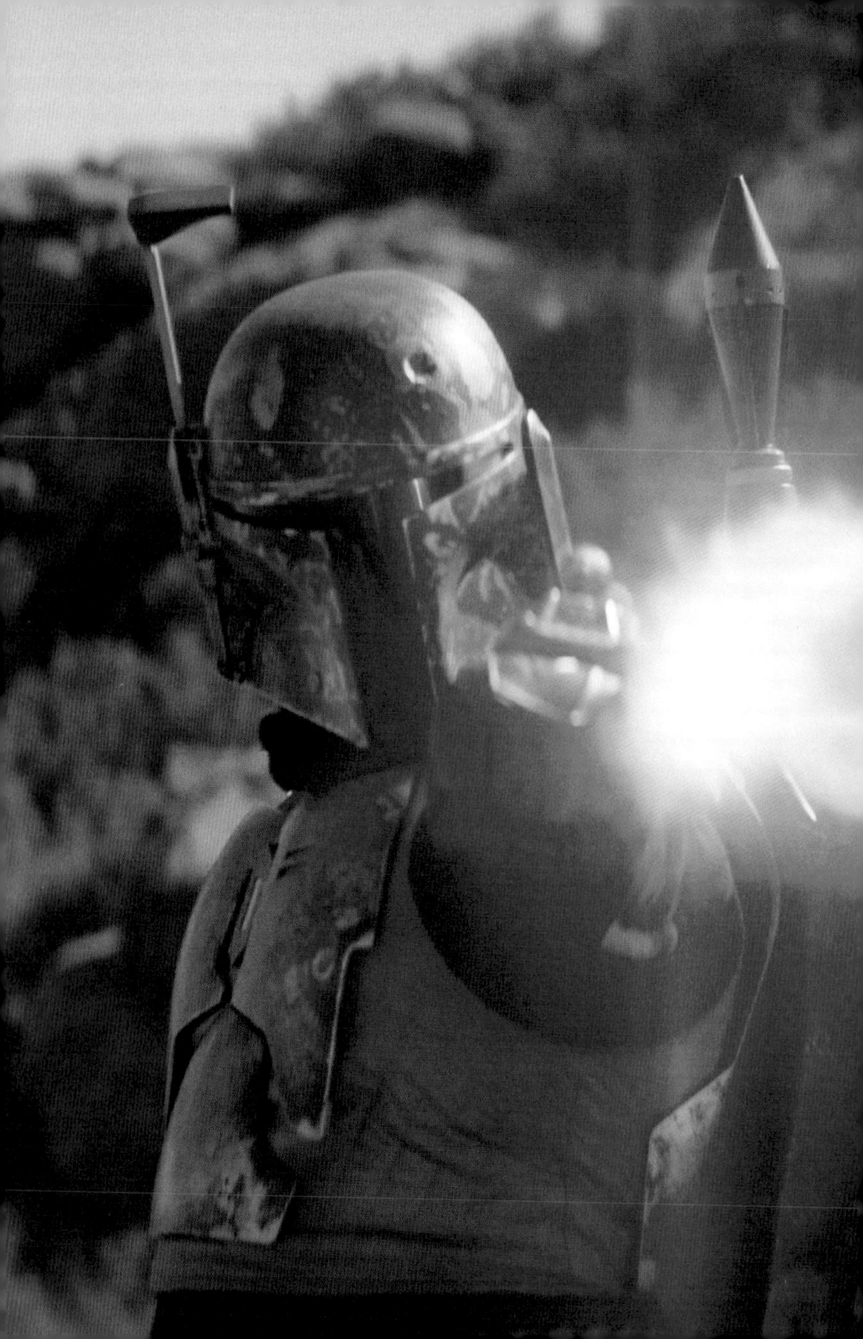

STAR WARS

BE MORE

BOBA FETT

Written by Joseph Jay Franco

Contents

Find your path 4

Be inspired 6

Seek out others like you 8

Don't get discouraged 10

There's a fine line between friend and frenemy 12

Figure out when to go solo 14

Work for hire 16

Never leave a deal on the table 18

Know when to subcontract 20

Don't get taken advantage of 22

Respect a worthy adversary 24

Always get paid 26

Stand out from the crowd 28

Don't make rookie mistakes 30

Dress for the job 32

Choose the best method of transportation 34

Outfit yourself with the right gear 36

Be bold 38

Master your trade 40

The only opinion that matters is the client's 42

Learn the many ways to skin a Loth-cat 44

Take pride in your work 46

Honor the terms of the deal 48

Remember that you're a freelancer 50

Play the long game 52

Bide your time 54

Have a contingency plan 56

Keep an eye on the competition 58

Keep your word, no matter what 60

Live to fight another day 62

Introduction

In an expansive galaxy you'll find every personality type. There are those who want to work for a large, stable employer like the Imperial Navy, pushing buttons on a space cruiser. There are those who are content living the simple (but dull) life of a merchant or moisture farmer. And then there are those special few who long for the freelance life.

If you aren't afraid of grueling (and sometimes frowned-upon) work, traveling to exotic locations, and being your own boss, you may find guidance in the wise words of those who have been there before you. Let them guide you on your path to the independent life of the successful contractor.

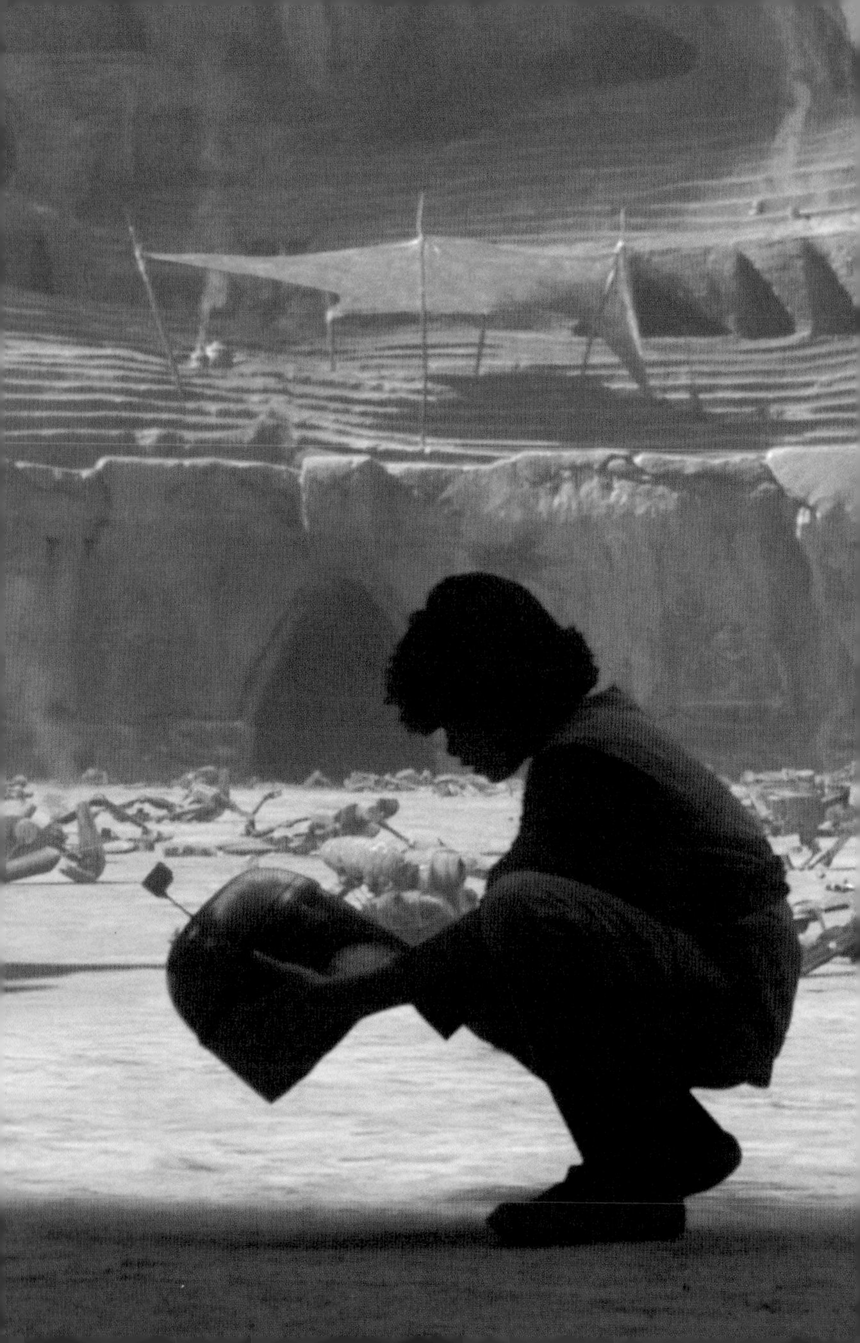

FIND YOUR PATH

One's path is not always clear. Choosing it is a big part of learning who you are and what you want to be. With dedication and focus, you can become that person—but it's going to take hard work. Be ready and willing to start at the bottom, to learn, and to take on every task with full commitment. All of it will build your experience and will one day make you a sought-after hire.

"Get him, Dad! Get him!"
Boba Fett

Be inspired

Identifying a role model in the field you'd like to get
into will give you something to aspire to, and help you
set goals to get there. Seek them out. Ask questions.
It might be a friend who has changed careers, or a
family member who became the template for a clone
army numbering in the millions. Just remember, even
if you want to be like them, you don't want to *be*
them. You must be true to yourself. Start by
networking to get an understanding of what
it takes to make it in your chosen field.

"Now relax, Boba is right..."
Aurra Sing

Seek out others like you

Early on, you may be totally on your own. That's OK, but if situations get tough, and you find yourself hung out to dry, you'll benefit from having others like you at your side. Those with the same ideals and goals, from whom you can learn and gain valuable experience. Sure, partnering up is risky, but it's also nice to know someone has your back. Working together to solve problems and complete the job can be a smart way to approach things.

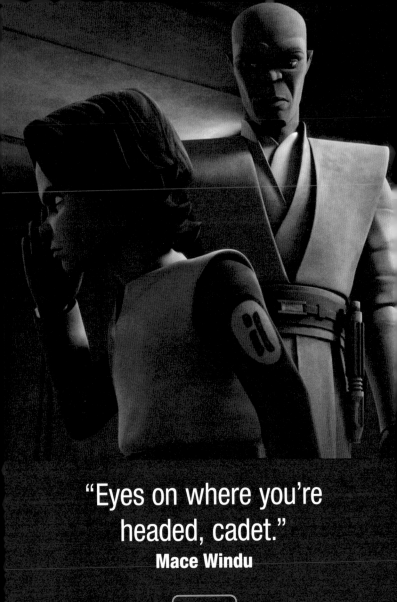

"Eyes on where you're
headed, cadet."
Mace Windu

Don't get discouraged

When you first start out, people may underestimate you.
Let them. This is a learning moment. Remember who
it was and bide your time. At some point you may get
the chance to show them what you can do. In a galaxy
filled with all sorts of smugglers, cheats, kingpins,
and overlords, a thick skin and long memory will be
essential not only for your survival but in building
the foundations of your career.

"Don't leave me. No!"
Boba Fett

There's a fine line between friend and frenemy

Many people will offer to help you along the way. Some are genuine, some will be fair-weather friends, and others will be no good. Learning to be an accurate judge of character is something that takes a lifetime to master. Some never get it right, but if you're working as a contractor you'll need to develop this skill. It can mean the difference between thriving in a competitive field or trading with Jawas—and nobody wants to make a living that way.

"You're too good for us now, is that it?"
Bossk

Figure out when to go solo

It's all fine and good to make friends and colleagues along the way, but when you're working for yourself, it is critical to know when to leave the group behind and head out on your own. If you've amassed enough connections and references to branch out, and you're spending more time fixing other people's mistakes than you're saving by teaming up, it's time to say goodbye and look ahead to the future—your future.

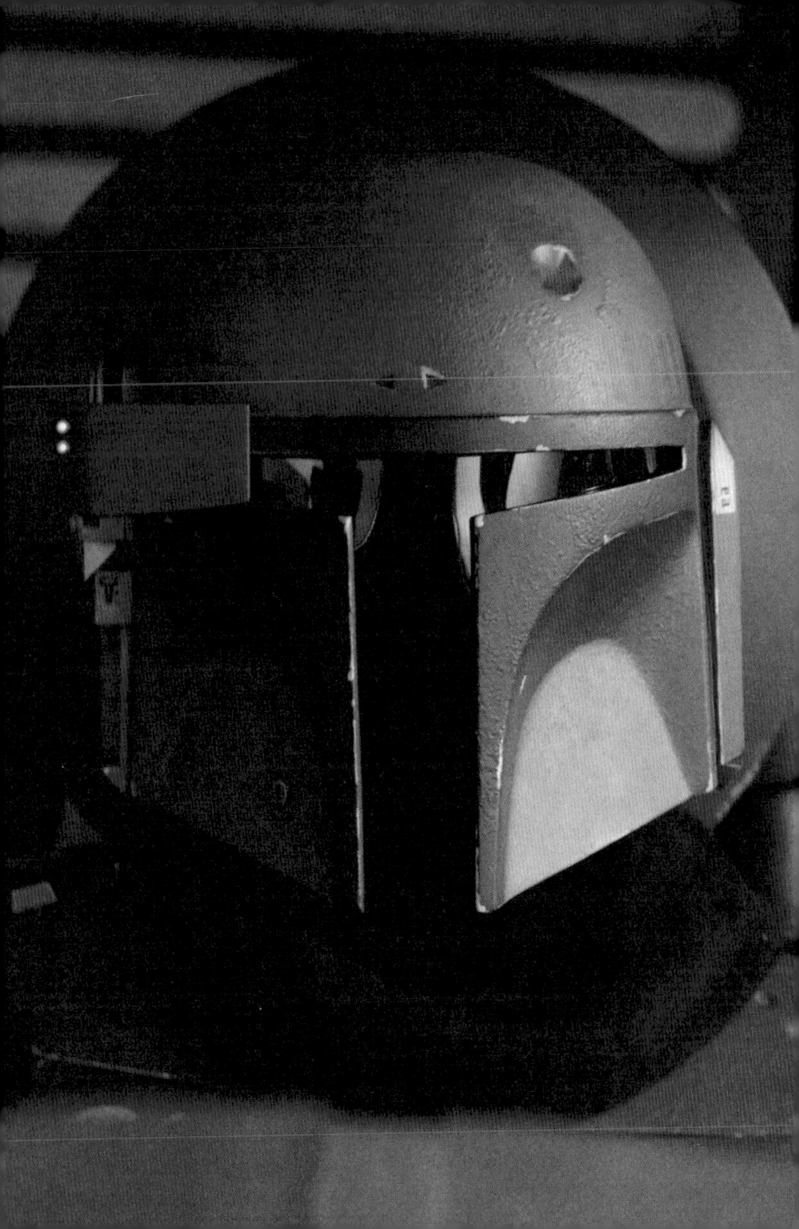

WORK FOR HIRE

The next step is getting out there and finding work. The only way to gain valuable experience in any field is to get your hands dirty. Experience is earned, not given out freely. This is not the time to be picky—this is the time to get out there and amass some battle scars, dents, and dings, all true signs of real-world experience.

"We would be honored if
you would join us."
Darth Vader

Never leave a deal on the table

Work hard, keep your head down, and be grateful
for the job: the galaxy doesn't owe you anything.
At this early stage you're not in a position to be picky.
When a potential employer asks you to be part of their
master plan, seize the opportunity and watch the credits
roll in. Learning how to read the room is important,
though. Sometimes you'll be expected to step up and
take action yourself, but sometimes you should let
the client take the lead.

"We'll have to try something more subtle this time, Zam. My client is getting impatient."

Jango Fett

Know when to subcontract

Most of the time, getting the work done yourself is best, since you know you can trust your own abilities. There may be other times, however, when it best suits you to distance yourself from a project, even if you're the one pulling the strings. A level or two of distance will allow you to focus on your overall game plan. Be cautious, though, because if things go sideways you may have to deal with both the person you hired and the one who hired you. Make sure it works for you before burning the blaster at both ends.

"I am altering the deal.
Pray I don't alter it any further."
Darth Vader

Don't get taken advantage of

It takes time to build a name for yourself, so stay focused. There will always be more work down the road if you hustle. But if you get in over your head things will quickly fall apart. With an established name, you may find yourself working for powerful people (or Hutts). Your assignment may be part of a much larger goal or target to meet. Make sure your voice isn't lost in the greater scheme of things. Position yourself to demand respect because of the quality of your work, and your deals won't get altered.

"Always a pleasure to
meet a Jedi."
Jango Fett

Respect a worthy adversary

As you reach a certain level of fame (or infamy) and build a reputation for reliability, don't rest on your laurels. There will always be someone at your heels thinking they can best you. If you're the one getting all the attention, it's easy to lose sight of those not far behind trying to overtake you. You will need to be scrappy, tenacious, and relentless to be the best. Sure, there might be some out there to be feared, like a well-trained Jedi, but with discipline and preparation you will be able to handle it.

"What if he doesn't survive?
He's worth a lot to me."
Boba Fett

Always get paid

Even if the client promises they will compensate you, it is important to clearly state your expectations and good practice to speak up for yourself. Although doing contract work can often make you feel like a small cog in a big machine, it is important to stand your ground, even in the face of a Dark Lord of the Sith. There is a fine line between being one of a million and being one *in* a million.

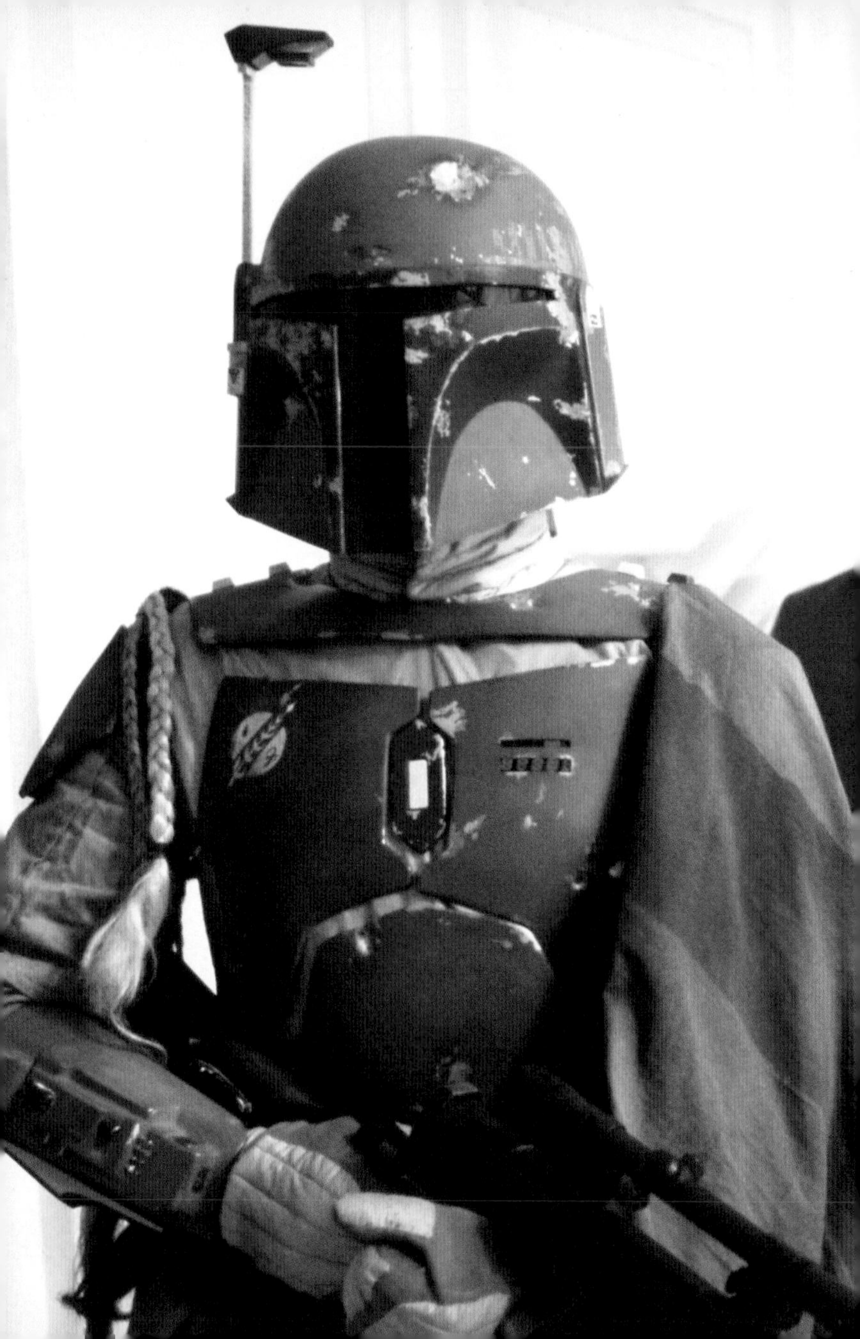

STAND OUT FROM THE CROWD

In any line of work there are competitors you'll have to vie with for business. They'll come in all shapes and sizes and have varying degrees of experience. Don't be deterred by them, just stay focused on the pathway ahead, eyes zeroed in on the prize. You need to show that you're different—better than the rest.

"I've been looking forward
to this for a long time."
Greedo

Don't make rookie mistakes

Your enthusiasm for the job will help carry you through these early days, when your experience is low and your contacts are few. But that enthusiasm can also make you vulnerable. Veteran freelancers will be able to spot you a mile off, so be on your guard. It's good to be bold, but don't get reckless, and be especially careful if a job pits you against someone with more experience.

"The armor was my father's!
Now, it's mine."
Boba Fett

Dress for the job

To properly dress for the job you'll need to know which outfit is best suited to the work. Will you be exposed to the elements, in an Imperial war room, or surrounded by the stench of Jabba's palace? Your signature look also needs to speak of your personal history, project an air of success, and be a reflection of your hard-earned victories. Make yours memorable, whether that's with a flashy tie or by sporting iconic armor recognized throughout the galaxy.

"Put Captain Solo
in the cargo hold."
Boba Fett

Choose the best method of transportation

Hitching a ride on public transport might be a cost-effective option at the start, but it doesn't afford you the flexibility that comes from having your own ride. If your work is going to have you dashing around the Outer Rim or engaging in clandestine reconnaissance missions, it's best to save up for your own vehicle. Whether it's a hand-me-down that needs some work or a Corellian freighter won in a game of sabacc, aim to keep that vehicle running and upgrade it as the credits allow.

"I gotta get one of those."
Din Djarin

Outfit yourself with the right gear

If you want to go into freelancing, it's important to become a master of all trades and tools. Sometimes getting your hands dirty like a common pit droid is the only way to learn how something works. Your personal equipment should reflect what you're most comfortable using and what will give you the most flexibility on any given job. Additionally, the more expensive and extensive your gear, the more successful you will appear to potential clients.

"Because he's holding a thermal detonator!"

C-3PO

Be bold

In a competitive marketplace, those who are bold
enough to take big risks earn big rewards. Some
opportunities might be too much for the average
contractor, but you want to make it so that no job is
too hard for you to handle. This might mean taking
the really tough assignment, accepting a seemingly
impossible task, or simply standing eye to eye with a
giant slug who enjoys watching gruesome executions.
Show no fear and go for the big jobs—you will be
rewarded in the end.

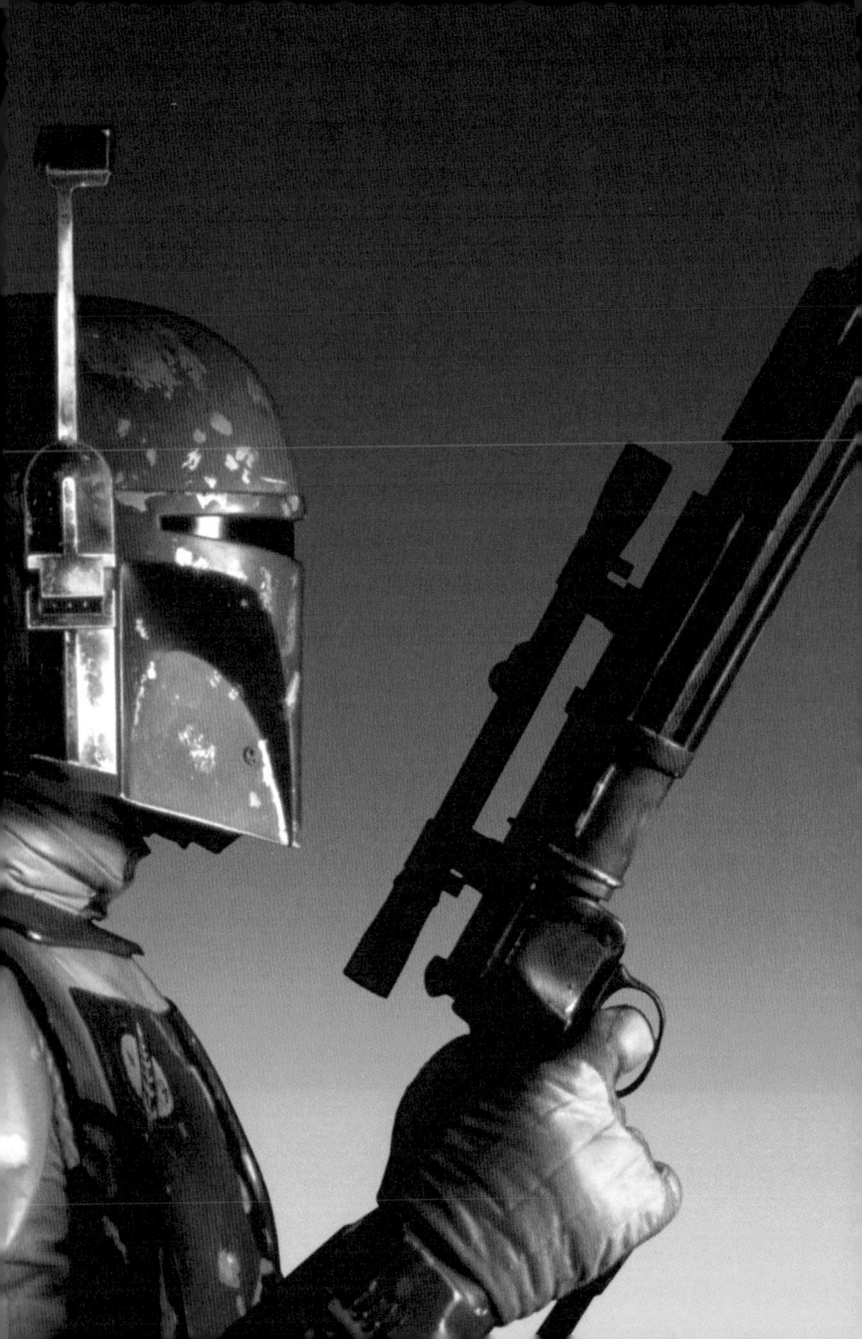

MASTER YOUR TRADE

You are no longer a rookie. When you walk into the room there is an audible silence and people tense up. Maybe they sweat a little. Your presence in any situation changes the game significantly. You may still need to outperform all others in your field to become the most sought-after specialist, but that is something you can handle.

"Bounty hunters?
We don't need that scum."
Admiral Piett

The only opinion that matters is the client's

As you go out on your own, you may have to associate with some questionable characters, but remember that your appearance, your reputation, and your skills are your own. Make use of what you were taught and build on each experience (or bounty) you take on. Many of the people you meet will respect the skills and experience offered by independent contractors, but some others may look down on you. Just remember: If they're not the one compensating you, pay them no mind.

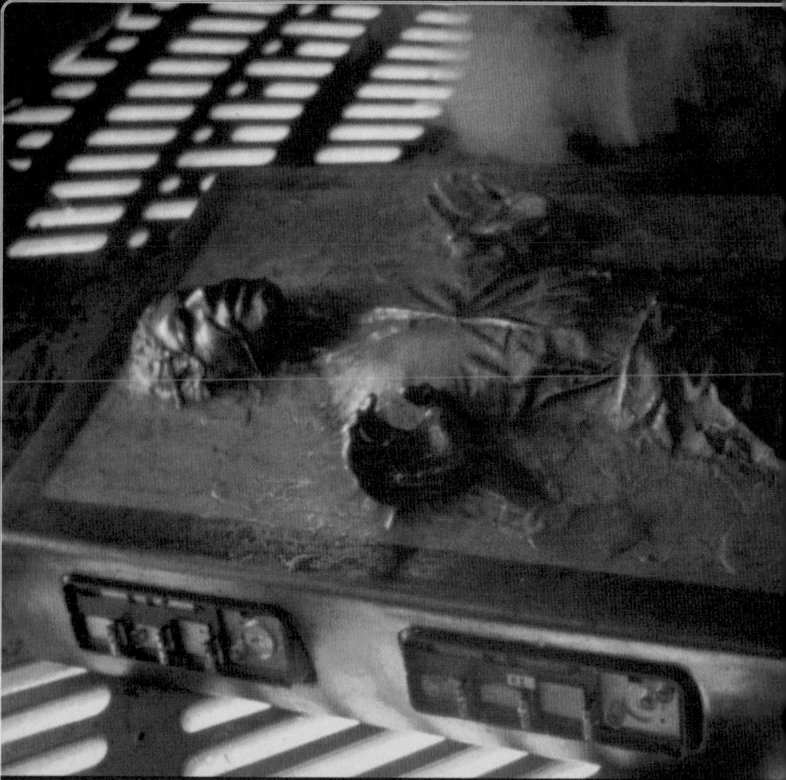

"Oh, they've encased him in carbonite, he should be quite well protected... if he survived the freezing process, that is."

C-3PO

Learn the many ways to skin a Loth-cat

Be open to unforeseen variables on any assignment, as what at first might seem like a potential problem could actually offer alternate ways to get the job done. Sometimes a risky maneuver can turn into an unexpected opportunity, save time, or reduce costs —setting up your own carbon-freezing chamber can get very pricey, but if there's one ready and waiting for you at the job site, why not use it?

"Well, if that isn't the quacta calling the stifling slimy."
Boba Fett

Take pride in your work

You should take pride in your accomplishments,
especially those that were hard won. Word of mouth
can be very beneficial, especially if you continue to
deliver and outperform others in your profession, so
stand up for yourself if competitors try to undermine
you. There is nothing wrong with displaying your
trophies, awards, or accolades, especially if it
leads to another gig.

"You are free to use any methods necessary, but I want them alive. No disintegrations!"

Darth Vader

Honor the terms of the deal

It will benefit you to know who you're dealing with. Idle threats from a cantina owner are very different to those from the Emperor's personal enforcer. Learn how much leeway you have on a given job and tread lightly. Do your homework by researching the potential employer, the job itself, and whatever other variables you can zero in on. Sometimes being given the freedom to use "any methods necessary" comes with conditions. Make sure you understand the terms of your agreement down to the letter.

"I give my allegiance
to no one."
Boba Fett

Remember that you're a freelancer

Whether working for the Empire or a thuggish gangster who lives in the middle of the desert, always remember that you're a hired gun. There are pros and cons that come with that, so use them to your advantage. Sure, you won't get invited to department meetings or the staff office party, but that's OK. It means you're free to focus on growing your own network of contacts across the galaxy.

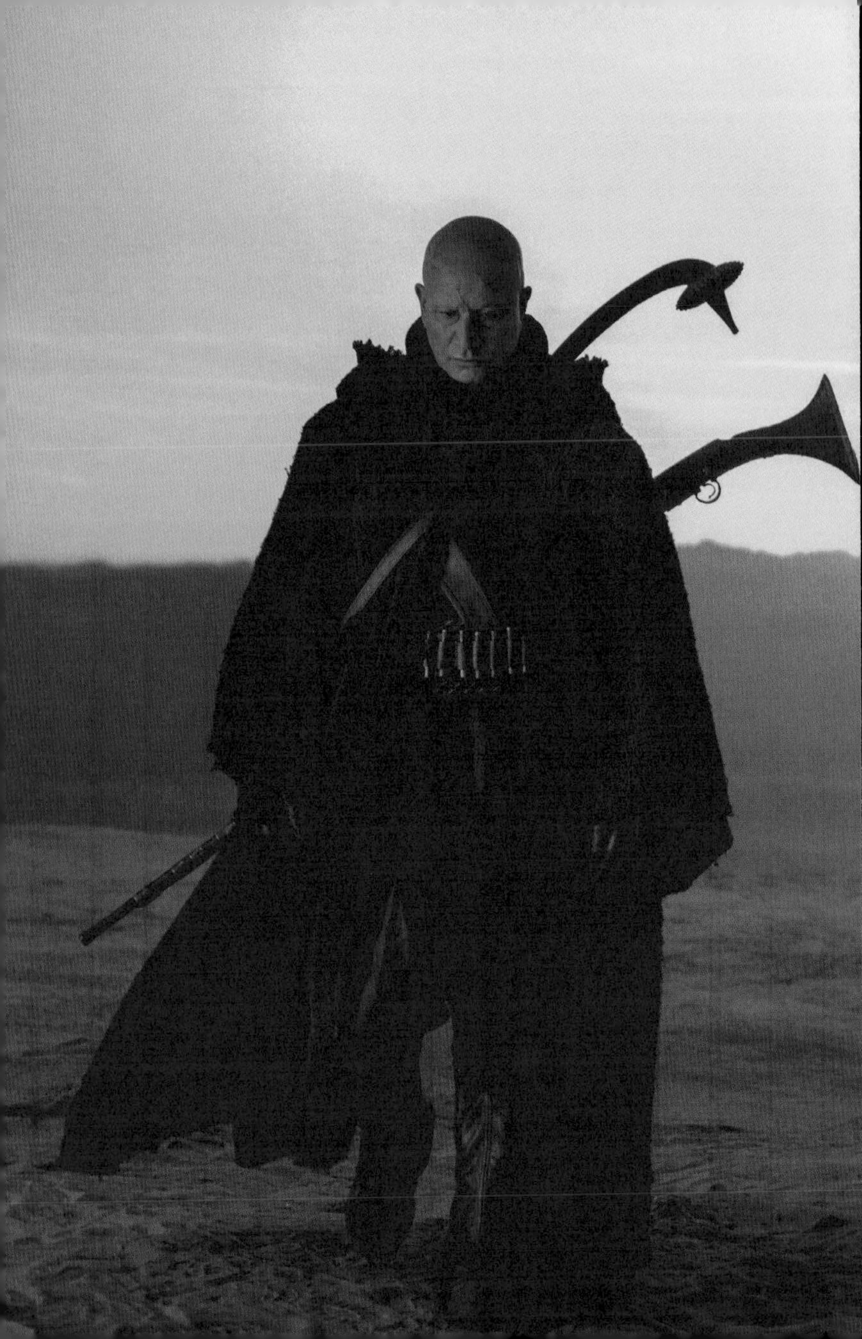

PLAY THE LONG GAME

Someone once said, "I'm just a simple man trying to make his way in the universe," and that sounds like solid advice. Avoid distractions, do your work, and keep to yourself. It may often feel like the galaxy has it in for you, but learning to get up after being knocked down will get you far in work and in life.

"I've been tracking you,
Mandalorian."
Boba Fett

Bide your time

By this stage of your career, you can afford to take
your time when assessing a situation before you
make any important decisions. Planning ahead is
sensible, whether that entails hiding your vessel from
smugglers or Jawas, or having a backup stash of
supplies. If you have to take on some work that you
feel is beneath you, do what you must to stay afloat and
eventually the time to rise again will present itself.

"Boba Fett? Boba Fett?! Where?"
Han Solo

Have a contingency plan

On any given job, no matter how much you prepare,
expect something—or everything—to go wrong.
It happens even to the best, but what sets you apart
is being ready for it and reacting fast. What if a
half-blind smuggler slammed your jetpack into
malfunction, causing you to get eaten by a giant,
pit-dwelling monster? Would you know what to do
next? Be ready for every worst-case scenario and
you'll have nothing to fear.

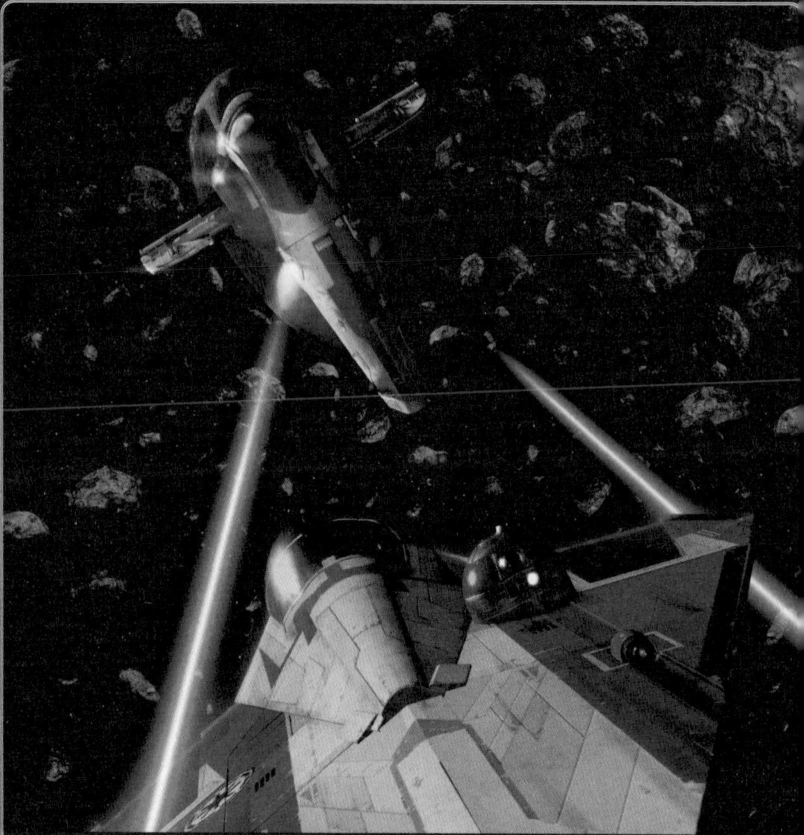

"He must have put a homing device on our hull. Hang on, son. We'll move into the asteroid field. And we'll have a couple of surprises for him."

Jango Fett

Keep an eye on the competition

Be careful not to become the hunted. As your career matures it's easy to get complacent, let your guard down, and ease up. Especially in the freelance marketplace, rivals will look for any gaps in your armor and then find ways to steal your business and leave you in the dust. On the plus side, having an arch-enemy might bring out the best in you by forcing you to raise your game and compete at a higher level.

"Until he's returned to you safely, we are in your debt."

Keep your word, no matter what

If you make a promise it is important to keep it.
Nobody wants to work with someone they can't trust,
and your word will mean nothing if you don't meet
your obligations. Whether dealing with powerful
figures not to be crossed, or backroom denizens of
low reputation, it's always better to under-promise
and over-deliver.

"I'm a simple man making his way through the galaxy. Like my father before me."

Boba Fett

Live to fight another day

With determination and hard work, you can achieve your goals. Having one eye on the short term is great for building your career, but some attention must be given to the future. Are you racing toward an early retirement or happy to enjoy a long and fruitful career in the Outer Rim? These are things to ponder. And if you get knocked out of the game and disappear for a while, you can always claw your way back and start again.

Senior Editor David Fentiman
Project Art Editor Jon Hall
Senior Production Editor Jennifer Murray
Senior Production Controller Mary Slater
Managing Editor Sarah Harland
Managing Art Editor Vicky Short
Publishing Director Mark Searle

DK would like to thank: Brett Rector and Michael Siglain at Lucasfilm Publishing;
Leland Chee, Pablo Hidalgo, and Kate Izquierdo at Lucasfilm Story Group;
Phil Szostak at Lucasfilm Art Department; Chelsea Alon at Disney Publishing;
and Julia March for proofreading.

First American Edition, 2021
Published in the United States by DK Publishing
1450 Broadway, Suite 801, New York, NY 10018

Page design copyright © 2021 Dorling Kindersley Limited
DK, a Division of Penguin Random House LLC
22 23 24 25 10 9 8 7 6 5 4 3 2
002–327338–Dec/2021

© & TM 2021 LUCASFILM LTD.

A catalog record for this book is available from the Library of Congress.
ISBN 978-0-7440-5316-6

DK books are available at special discounts when purchased in bulk for sales
promotions, premiums, fund-raising, or educational use. For details, contact:
DK Publishing Special Markets, 1450 Broadway, Suite 801, New York, NY 10018.
SpecialSales@dk.com

Printed and bound in Canada

For the curious
www.dk.com

www.starwars.com

MIX
Paper from
responsible sources
FSC™ C018179

This book was made with Forest
Stewardship Council ™ certified
paper—one small step in DK's
commitment to a sustainable
future. For more information go to
www.dk.com/our-green-pledge

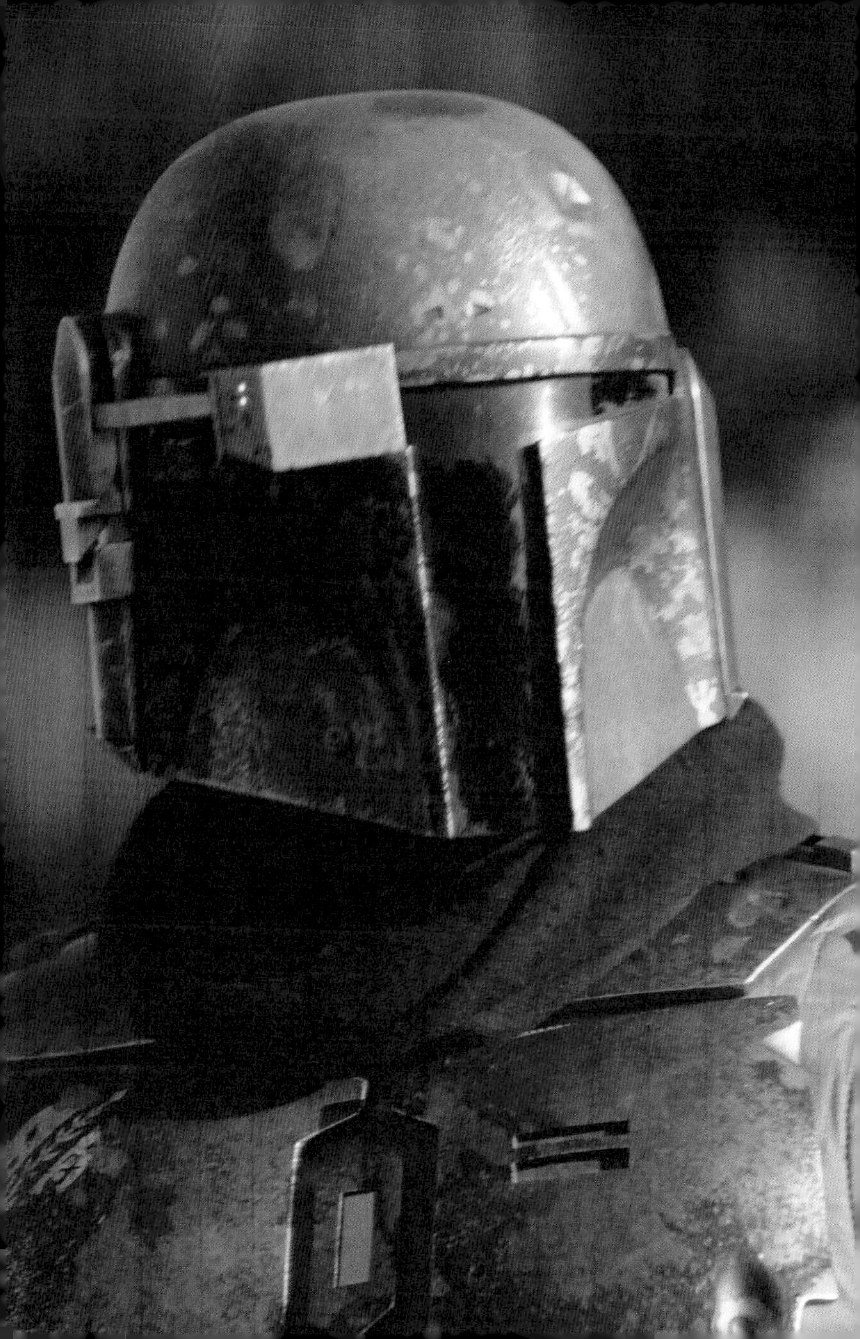

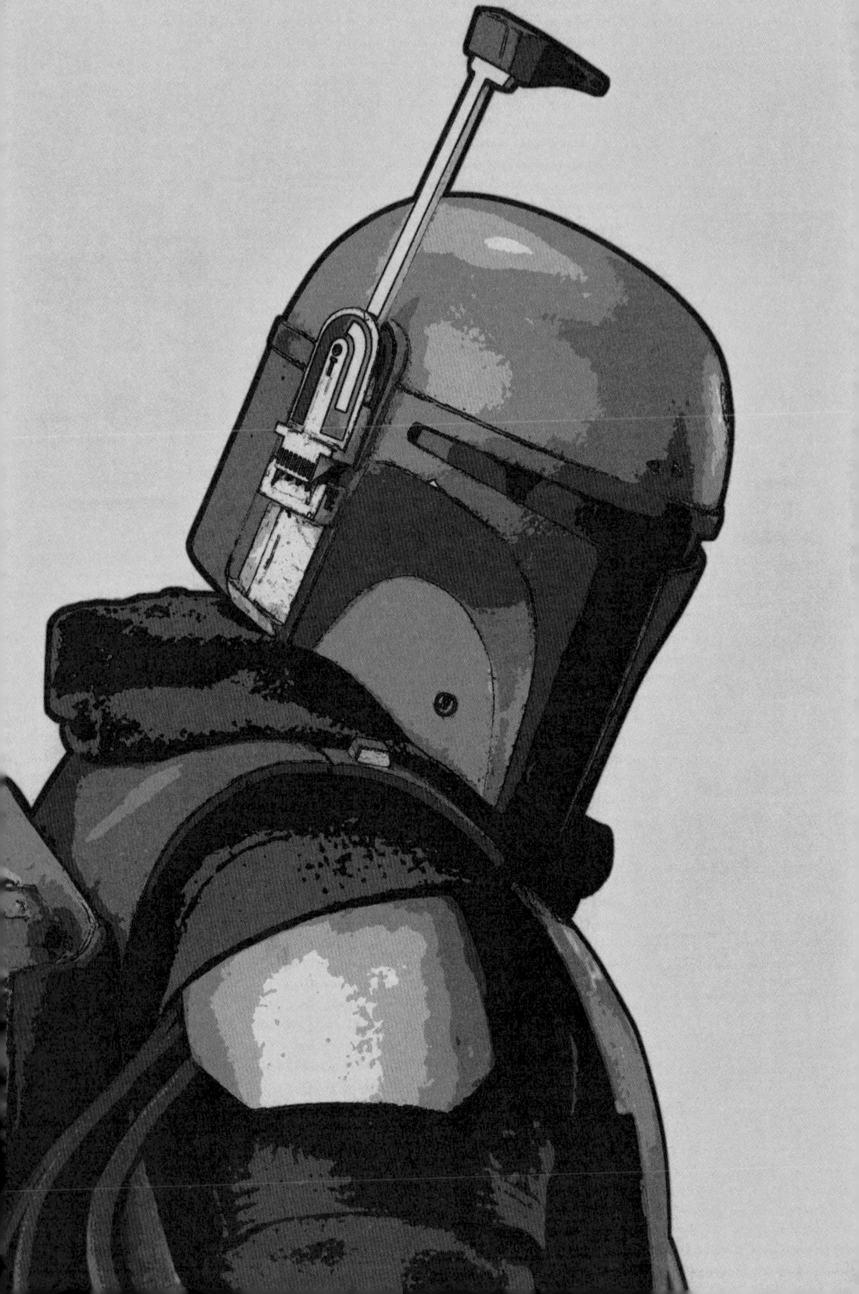